I0454563

The Insider's Guide to Business Credit Using an EIN Only:

Get Tradelines, Credit Cards, and Loans for Your Business with No Personal Guarantee

Alyssa Garner and Garrett Garner

Copyright © 2023 Alyssa Garner and Garrett Garner
All rights reserved

No part of this publication may be reproduced or transmitted in any form or by any means, electronic or mechanical, including photography, recording, or any information storage and retrieval system without the prior written consent from the publisher and author, except in the instance of quotes for reviews. No part of this book may be uploaded without the permission of the publisher and author, nor be otherwise circulated in any form of binding or cover other than that in which it is originally published

The publisher and author acknowledge the trademark status and trademark ownership of all trademarks, service marks and word marks mentioned in this book.

Disclaimer

The information in this book is for informational and educational purposes only. It should not be construed as business, tax, or legal advice of any kind. All information and resources found in this book are based on the opinions of the authors alone unless otherwise noted.

The authors of this book assume no responsibility or liability for any consequence resulting directly or indirectly from any action or inaction you take based on the information found in this book.

While the authors have made every effort to provide accurate information at the time of publication, they do not assume any responsibility for errors or changes that occur after publication.

This book is intended to be used only as a general guide, and not as a sole source of information on the subject matter. Always consult a licensed professional before attempting any techniques outlined in this book.

Congrats!

Congratulations on picking up this book! You currently hold in your hands the keys to successfully obtaining tradelines using an EIN only.

We're SO excited to hear what you think! Once you've finished the book, we would love it if you'd leave an honest review on Amazon.

Your review provides valuable feedback and helps us bring more books and resources to you. We appreciate your support!

Contents

Introduction

All businesses need funding to grow. This means access to business credit.

While smaller businesses generally need this funding the most, they're often the ones who struggle the most to get it.

This doesn't sound fair, does it? Well, we're here to even the playing field.

We've written this book to help ALL business owners access the business credit they need to be successful—regardless of the size of the business or how long it's been operational.

No matter where you are in your business journey, you CAN obtain business tradelines and boost your business credit score without putting your personal assets at risk!

This book will teach you exactly how to build credit in your business's name, including receiving access to trade credit, credit cards, and business loans, with NO personal guarantee needed from you as the business owner.

To do this, you'll use an Employer Identification Number (EIN) to apply for business credit instead of your Social Security Number (SSN). In doing so, you'll boost your business credit score and reputation, while keeping your business and personal finances separate.

This is a wise move for business owners because it prevents any financial issues in your business from affecting your personal credit. It limits your personal liability and can help you achieve more favorable terms when you apply for personal credit cards or loans.

In this book, we'll teach you exactly how to set up your business in such a way that will make receiving business credit a breeze instead of a chore. You'll learn the exact steps for increasing your business's fundability, accessing your business credit reports, and establishing multiple tradelines quickly.

Once your business is properly set up for funding, you can receive business credit in as little as 24–48 hours, boost your business credit score (even if you don't have one yet), and receive business credit cards and loans with just your EIN—no personal guarantee needed.

This book will show you exactly how to achieve all this quickly with our simple step-by-step framework. Ready to get started?

CHAPTER 1

Business Structure

First things first, you'll want to make sure that your business is properly set up to receive funding.

If you want to keep your business and personal finances (and credit scores) separate, you'll need two things: (1) a separate business entity and (2) an EIN. If you already have these, feel free to just skim this chapter or skip ahead to chapter 2.

Business Entity

When you first start a business, the default business type is a sole proprietorship, which does NOT create a legal separation between the business owner and their business. This means you'll still be personally liable for any debt your business accumulates.

In order to avoid this, you'll need to instead create a business entity that is separate from you, as the owner. For most small businesses, this is best achieved through forming a limited liability company, or LLC.

While the primary purpose of an LLC is to maintain a legal separation between your personal and business assets, there are other benefits as well, including pass-through taxation and the ability to open a business bank account.

Pass-through taxation means business income is only taxed once at the individual level, which ensures that you won't be taxed twice. This can result in significant tax savings for your business.

Setting up an LLC is easier and cheaper than most people think. It generally costs $100–$300 per year to maintain (depending on the state) and the tax benefits usually more than make up for this cost.

Below is the basic step-by-step process for setting up an LLC. This process can vary a bit by state, so make sure you do your own research and consult a professional whenever necessary.

1. Choose a name for your LLC.

Be sure that the name is available and fits within the naming guidelines for your state. If your LLC is a different name than the one your business is operating under, you will also need a "doing business as" (DBA) or trade name. This is a simple process that just requires an additional form.

2. Choose a resident agent in your state.

All states require a resident agent when forming an LLC. This is a person or business entity that accepts tax and legal documents on behalf of your business.

3. File the articles of organization with your state.

This is a simple form that you fill out and mail to the designated department in your state along with any associated fees. They are also sometimes called articles of incorporation.

For most businesses just starting out, an LLC is the most logical choice for creating a separate business entity that will allow you to receive tradelines without affecting your personal finances.

Another option for forming a separate business entity is a corporation. There are several different types and they are oftentimes a bit trickier to set up and manage, so we recommend consulting with an attorney or other legal expert for this.

EIN

Once you've formed your LLC, you can apply for your Employer Identification Number, or EIN. This is a nine-digit number assigned to a business entity by the IRS. It's also sometimes referred to as a Federal Tax Identification Number.

You'll use your EIN to apply for business credit and loans instead of your SSN. This will allow you to receive business funding without the need for a personal guarantee.

You can apply for an EIN online by visiting this website: irs.gov/businesses/small-businesses-self-employed/employer-id-numbers

The application will ask for the approved legal name of your business and the date it was formed. For this reason, we recommend that you form your LLC first before applying for an EIN.

If no issues arise, you can receive your EIN immediately upon completing the application. This is the first step toward building your business credit profile and obtaining tradelines without a personal guarantee.

CHAPTER 2

Fundability

Once you have your LLC and EIN, the next step is to create a professional and creditworthy business presence. The main goal here is to have creditors and lenders recognize your business as a fundable entity separate from the owner.

When you apply for business credit, creditors and lenders will look into and research your company to determine how fundable your business is. It's important for your business to appear both presentable and congruent on all fronts, so you can receive credit and loans without issue.

Business Presence

In this section, we'll provide a list of must-have business essentials that, when properly set up, will ensure fundability in the eyes of potential creditors, lenders, and vendors.

Business Address

Your company needs a physical and deliverable address in order to be considered for business credit. If you have a physical business location that is separate from your home, this is ideal.

If you operate an online or home-based business, you may be tempted to choose your home address as your company address. This can work in a pinch, but it's preferable to have a separate physical address, if possible (PO boxes aren't allowed).

If your business operates out of your home, you can consider a coworking space, a registered agent with a physical office, or a virtual business address provider (such as Alliance Virtual Offices or Regus) as your official business address. There may be a few cases where lenders won't accept these alternatives, but it's still generally better than using your home address.

If you choose to use your home address, you can typically still receive funding, but be prepared for lenders to ask more questions and for them to look deeper into your business to ensure its fundability.

Business Phone Number

A dedicated phone number legitimizes your business and is something creditors like to see. Make sure this phone number is listed with 411 directory assistance (many lenders will check this) by calling your local phone service provider or visiting listyourself.net/ListYourself.

If you don't have a business phone, you can use a service like GoDaddy Conversations to add a business phone number to your cell phone. You can also increase your business's legitimacy by adding a toll-free number through your phone service provider.

Website

Potential creditors will often research your business online, so it's essential to have a professional and informative website for them to find.

To create a professional website, you'll need a domain name (the URL for your business), web hosting, and a website builder. We recommend

Squarespace or Wix as easy and affordable options. At a minimum, your website should list the products or services you offer and your contact information.

Email Address

Similar to a phone number, a company email address legitimizes your business in the eyes of creditors.

It's best to have an email address that uses your domain name (e.g., alyssa@yogacandles.com), as opposed to just a Gmail address, as it appears more professional. If you have a website, you can use your domain name to create a custom email address.

Google Business Profile

This is a free tool that allows you to manage the information that shows up for your company on Google. It also creates better visibility for your business and helps you rank in local search results.

Social Media

While not strictly required, social media pages for your business on platforms such as LinkedIn or Facebook can also help your business appear more legitimate.

Consistency

Once you have all of the above, the most important thing is to ensure consistency. Check to make sure that your business details are listed EXACTLY the same everywhere, including with the IRS, your bank, and 411 directory assistance, as well as on business licenses, bills, and invoices.

As an example, your business name and address on your website should perfectly match your business name and address on the Secretary of State's website. This includes small details, such as using an ampersand (&) versus the word "and" or the use of punctuation marks.

It's very important to maintain consistency, as even small discrepancies can lead to your application being marked as fraudulent. Don't let this happen to you!

Be diligent and make sure your business information is listed precisely the same every time. Keep an exact record of how this information is written and then simply copy and paste to guarantee no errors.

By following the guidance in this chapter, you will ensure that your business appears professional and consistent, which will drastically increase your fundability. This will help you receive more tradelines and higher limits when you apply for business credit in chapter 4.

CHAPTER 3

Credit Reports

Now that your business is properly set up, it's time to access your business credit reports. These are offered by Dun & Bradstreet (D&B), Experian, and Equifax—the three major business credit bureaus.

When it comes to receiving business credit, knowing your credit score and monitoring your reports is an essential component. In fact, the Nav American Dream Gap survey found that small business owners who know their business credit score are 41% more likely to be approved for a loan.

By understanding how to access and monitor your business credit reports, you'll already be ahead of the pack and ready to receive business credit in the next chapter.

Business Identifier

The first step is to get a free DUNS number from D&B. This is D&B's own business identifier and it will show up on your D&B credit report. You can request your DUNS number by going to dnb.com/duns/get-a-duns.html.

Experian and Equifax issue business identifiers as well, but you don't generally need to request these, as they'll be assigned when you register your business with the state.

Business Profile

To start, you'll want to make sure your business profile is set up properly with each credit bureau. As we mentioned in the previous chapter, it's important for your business details to be an exact match everywhere—this includes your business credit reports and profiles.

Here's where to update your company information with each credit bureau:

- For D&B, go to dnb.com/duns-number/view-update-company-credit-file.html.

- For Experian and Equifax, company information on your business credit report comes directly from the creditors. When you update your information with creditors, the change will generally be applied to Experian and Equifax, as well. If there is incorrect information on your report, you can open up a dispute online with either bureau.

D&B Business Listing also allows you to add additional information to your company's profile page in the D&B Directory. They have a free listing that allows you to add hours of operation, languages, social media URLs, and payment methods. This gives your business more exposure and helps you maintain a consistent business identity.

If you'd like to add additional information to your listing, such as a company description, tagline, or logo, you can pay to purchase a Basic or Plus listing. This isn't at all necessary, but can be helpful if your business can afford it.

There are companies that offer no personal guarantee business credit cards and extend credit by invitation only. Adding as much information as possible to your D&B Business Listing can help you gain access to these opportunities.

Credit Reports

Next, you'll want to check and begin monitoring your business credit reports and scores.

Unlike personal credit reports, there is a fee associated with checking your business credit report with the major bureaus. Luckily, there are also some free ways to access and monitor your score and other information on your report. We'll explore both paid and free options throughout the following sections.

Remember that your business credit reports and scores are completely separate from your personal ones.

D&B

With D&B, you can pay $39 a month for their CreditMonitor plan, which offers the ability to monitor your business credit file in real time. You'll receive unlimited access to all your scores and ratings, as well as detailed explanations of these metrics.

While this is a great service, small businesses don't necessarily need all of the features offered in CreditMonitor. As an alternative, CreditSignal Plus is $15 a month and gives you unlimited access to five business credit scores, as well as email alerts of any changes.

D&B also offers a free service called CreditSignal that allows you to view four scores and receive some email alerts as well. The biggest downside is that access to the free program is only good for 14 days.

Experian

With Experian, you can pay a one-time charge of $39.95 to view your business credit scores and profile through CreditScore Report. While this will help you understand your current scores, you won't be able to monitor them or check your progress over time.

Paying the one-time fee multiple times does add up, so we recommend Business Credit Advantage, which gives you unlimited access to your scores, credit alerts, ongoing tracking, and more for $189 per year. It's the best way to monitor your Experian scores over time.

Equifax

With Equifax, you can order a single business credit report by contacting them through their website. They don't have prices listed, as it depends on your individual business and the type of report.

While accessing your Equifax report can be useful, it's not as necessary to keep tabs on as your D&B and Experian scores.

Nav

Nav offers a service that provides a summary of your business credit reports for free. You won't receive direct access to reports and scores as you would through the credit bureaus, but the information is still useful and will give you a general sense of your scores and progress.

Tillful

Tillful is a mobile app that offers business credit summaries, scores, and a health score for free. They are now part of Nav and offer many of the same features. They've also partnered with Experian and can provide your Intelliscore Plus for free.

Regardless of which of the above options you choose, be sure to monitor your business credit reports regularly. It's important to be aware of your latest score and to check your progress. You should also ensure that your payment history and credit utilization are correct, and there is no fraudulent activity on your report.

While you can use the free services alone, we do recommend setting up D&B's CreditSignal Plus ($15 per month) and Experian's Business Credit Advantage ($189 per year), at minimum, if you can afford it. These services are the most cost-effective way to consistently check and monitor your scores, so you can stay on track and be aware of your progress.

Score

One thing that's often confusing to those new to business credit is the score itself. Each credit bureau uses a variety of scoring ranges, so what's considered a "good" or "bad" score can be subjective.

While D&B offers more than five different business credit scores, the most important is the PAYDEX score. This measures payment history on a scale of 1–100.

Generally, a score of 80 or above is considered good and means that you're making on-time or early payments. You'll need a minimum of three tradelines (which we'll discuss in the next chapter) to establish a PAYDEX score.

Intelliscore Plus from Experian also offers scores between 1 and 100, but this score measures credit risk. A score between 76 and 100 would generally be considered "good" or low risk. This score is determined by your payment history, number of liens and judgments, and credit utilization.

Recently, Experian released an updated version of this score called Intelliscore Plus V3. This metric uses a scoring range of 300 to 850 and a good score would generally be 720 or higher. This updated score isn't widely used yet, but is likely to gain traction over time.

Once you have access to your reports, you can start building business credit by establishing tradelines with companies that report to D&B, Experian, and/or Equifax. We'll show you exactly how to do this in the following chapters.

Note that if your business is new and has no credit history yet, you may have to wait until after you've established your first few tradelines to access your business credit reports and set up credit monitoring.

CHAPTER 4

Your First Tradelines

Congrats! Your business structure, fundability, and credit reports are ready to go, so you can gain easy approval for your first tradelines.

This is the exciting part, where you'll start to receive credit for your business under your EIN with no personal guarantee or SSN required. It all starts with trade credit.

Trade credit, also known as vendor credit, is the fastest way to build your business credit profile and score. This will open doors for you to receive credit cards and loans using your EIN only later on.

Trade credit is a financing option that allows you to make purchases directly from a business without paying up front. In other words, you can place an order now, but you won't have to pay for a set amount of time.

Net 15, net 30, net 45, and net 60 are common payment terms for trade credit, which indicate that the bill is expected to be paid in full within the specified time frame. For example, net 30 on an invoice means you have 30 days to pay the vendor in full. Net 30 terms are most common for new businesses.

Once your application with a vendor is approved, you can typically select "net 30" at checkout. Your payment terms will be indicated on the invoice and there are sometimes incentives for paying early. As long as you pay the invoice by the indicated date, there will be no interest on the payment and you can start to positively build your business credit score.

There are two tiers of trade credit: tier 1 and tier 2. Tier 1 is basic trade credit for those who have little to no business credit history, while tier 2 is advanced trade credit for businesses with a positive and established credit history.

In this chapter, we'll present a list of vendors that issue tier 1 tradelines to new businesses and report to the major credit bureaus. Once you demonstrate a positive payment history in tier 1, you can apply for tier 2 tradelines, which we'll discuss in chapter 5.

Both tier 1 and tier 2 tradelines allow you to purchase useful products for your business, such as business plans, web design, or office supplies, on credit, while simultaneously building your business credit score and profile. It's a win-win!

These vendors don't require an SSN, so you can apply for credit using your EIN only. This allows you to receive credit quickly, while limiting your personal liability.

To apply for net 30 tradelines, most vendors will require the following information at a minimum:

- Legal business name
- Business address (must be identical on all documents)
- Phone number and email address (must be verifiable)
- EIN
- DUNS number

Once you've applied, most vendors will give you a decision in 24–48 hours and you can start building your business credit.

Keep in mind that the key here isn't just to establish tradelines with vendors, but specifically to establish tradelines with vendors that report to D&B, Experian, and/or Equifax. If a vendor doesn't report to a major credit bureau, even with early or on-time payments, you won't build your business credit score. All of the vendors on the list below report to at least one of the three major credit bureaus.

In the following pages, we'll present the best tier 1 vendor accounts with net 30 terms. While most of these are great even for brand-new businesses, a few have specific requirements that will be listed in their corresponding sections.

Note that some vendors require that you prepay for a certain amount of initial orders before you can fully utilize their net 30 terms. Many also have minimum order requirements for credit bureau reporting.

While we've made every effort to ensure that the information below is accurate at the time of writing, always check the vendor's website for the most up-to-date information.

Top Tier 1 Vendor Accounts (NO Personal Guarantee)

Wise Business Plans

Wise Business Plans is one of the easiest vendor accounts to be approved for as a new business. You simply fill out the application form online and remit a $99 annual fee.

As the name implies, they primarily sell business plans, which are essential for many businesses, as they are often required to receive bank loans or lease office spaces. They also have website design and branding services that could be very useful, especially for new companies.

Wise Business Plans net 30 accounts are reported monthly to Experian and Equifax.

Creative Analytics

Creative Analytics is another great vendor account for new companies, as businesses only need to be established for 30 days in order to qualify for their net 30 program. They offer a variety of digital marketing services, management consulting services, and physical products for businesses.

You can apply online with your EIN and DUNS number. They report to D&B and Equifax.

The annual fee is $79 per year with an initial credit limit of $1,000.

Branded Apparel Club (formerly Business T-Shirt Club)

This is a membership-based custom apparel printing company created for business owners and entrepreneurs. If your business requires branded or pre-decorated T-shirts, sweatshirts, accessories, or anything else, this net 30 vendor is a great option.

The annual membership fee is $69.99. A 50% deposit will be required on all orders for new members, but can be lifted after a minimum of five orders have been placed with on-time full payments.

Branded Apparel Club reports to Equifax.

NAMYNOT

NAMYNOT offers digital marketing services, including SEO, content writing, social media marketing, website design, and more—all of which are useful to businesses operating online.

They report payment history to D&B and offer credit limits up to $10,000. You can apply online through their website.

A huge benefit of NAMYNOT is, unlike many other vendors, there is no monthly or annual fee for net 30 accounts. There is also no order minimum for credit bureau reporting.

The only caveat is that your company must be established for at least 90 days to be considered. You also need to have a business website.

The CEO Creative

The CEO Creative is a great vendor account for both new and established businesses alike. They offer something for everyone, including office supplies, electronics, website development, and even home and office cleaning supplies.

The annual fee is $49 upon approval. Your business needs to be operational for at least 30 days. They also offer discounts for paying early (before your net 30 term is up).

The CEO Creative reports to both D&B and Experian.

ULINE

ULINE is great for all businesses, as trade credit is easy to establish and most companies will qualify.

They sell a large variety of packaging and shipping supplies, which makes ULINE an especially good option for those who have an Etsy shop, eBay store, or other e-commerce business. They also sell paper, cleaning supplies, office furniture, and more.

To apply, you simply hit "Invoice Me" during the checkout process. Just note that you will need the customer number from the back of a ULINE catalog, but you can easily request one for free on their website.

ULINE reports to D&B and Experian. There is no annual membership fee or minimum order requirement for credit bureau reporting, making it an ideal option for smaller businesses.

Crown Office Supplies

This vendor mainly sells office and school supplies, as well as some electronics and apparel. There is a $99 annual fee and your business must be established for at least 90 days.

Crown Office Supplies reports to D&B, Equifax, and Experian making it an ideal option for those who want to build business credit with all three major bureaus.

Summa Office Supplies

Summa sells office supplies (such as markers, labels, envelopes, and folders) alongside cloud-based and digital products (such as business software, guides, and courses).

They offer two tiers of net 30 credit:

- Tier 1 is more limited and only allows you to purchase digital products. All payments for purchases above $75 will be reported to Equifax.

- Tier 2 allows you to purchase physical products. All payments for purchases above $75 will be reported to D&B.

As discussed previously, a new business can only qualify for the tier 1 account since at least six months of credit history is needed for Summa's tier 2 program.

One distinct advantage of Summa is that they offer written trade credit references, which can help small business owners qualify for further financing. Some creditors are willing to accept trade credit references in lieu of a strong business credit score.

Shirtsy

Shirtsy sells apparel, business cards, mugs, magnets, and more—all customized to your brand. It's a great way to get the word out about your business, while also building your credit!

The annual fee is $99 and you must be in business for at least 30 days to qualify. Shirtsy reports to D&B, Experian, and Equifax, which helps build your credit profile with all three major bureaus.

Office Garner

Office Garner sells a wide variety of business supplies, including apparel, electronics, stationery, and even housewares and kitchen appliances.

They have a $69 annual fee and a minimum purchase amount of $45 for credit bureau reporting. Office Garner reports to D&B and Equifax.

They offer an initial credit limit of up to $1,500. After you pay three net 30 invoices in full, you can ask for a credit limit increase. Like Summa, Office Garner also provides trade references upon request.

Your First Tradeline

Now that you have our top 10 list of best tier 1 vendor accounts, it's time to apply for your first tradeline!

If you've followed the guidance from previous chapters and your business is set up properly for credit, you can often receive your first tradeline approval in 24–48 hours or less.

Remember to list the exact same business information (name, address, phone number, website, email address, etc.) on every application you fill out to ensure easy approval and no red flags. As noted in chapter 3, Experian and Equifax receive the company information listed on your business credit report directly from vendors and creditors, so it's extra important to ensure this is completely accurate down to the very last detail.

Once your first net 30 account reports to one of the three major credit bureaus, their system will automatically create your business credit file, if it isn't already established. From there, with early and on-time payments on your net 30 tradelines, you can watch your business credit grow!

After your first approval, you can start applying for other tier 1 vendor accounts. We recommend having at least 5–8 tier 1 tradelines reporting to the major credit bureaus. You'll build your business credit quickly this way, which will help you qualify for the tier 2 accounts we'll discuss in the next chapter.

Keep in mind that it's not enough just to have net 30 accounts in your business's name. Business credit is built through early and on-time payments on your accounts.

To that end, be sure to always pay the balance in full before the end of your payment term to increase your business credit score. As you establish a solid reputation for making purchases and paying on time, you may eventually be eligible for greater credit limits or longer net terms with your vendors.

Finally, keep in mind that a new vendor account can take up to 60 days to appear on your business credit reports. Be patient and know that you're improving your credit score, even if you can't see the impact right away.

CHAPTER 5

Increase Your Tradelines

In this chapter, we'll explore tier 2 vendor accounts, which is the next step in building your business credit score and profile.

Once you've acquired 5–8 tradelines with the tier 1 vendors listed in chapter 4 and demonstrated a positive credit history of on-time or early payments, you can start to apply to tier 2 vendor accounts.

Just like the tier 1 accounts in chapter 4, you can apply to our top tier 2 accounts using your EIN only with no personal guarantee. They will also report to at least one of the three major credit bureaus.

The main difference is that tier 2 vendors typically conduct a business credit check before extending credit. This means you must have a business credit history already established through your tier 1 vendor accounts. On the plus side, tier 2 programs provide higher credit limits, longer terms, and better perks. Some of these are vendor accounts, while others are issued as store credit cards.

For your best approval odds, we recommend having at least 5–8 tier 1 vendor accounts and at least 90 days of early or on-time payment history listed on your credit profile. Remember that it could take up to 60 days for new information to appear on your credit profile, so be sure to check your score and reports before applying.

The following is our list of recommended tier 2 vendors for continuing to build your business credit. You can apply to these using just your EIN with no personal guarantee required.

We recommend adding at least 2–5 tier 2 tradelines reporting to the major credit bureaus for a total of 10 or more tradelines on your credit file. Ideally, at least one of your accounts should have a credit limit of $10,000 or more.

As always, be sure to check the vendor websites for the most up-to-date information as program terms and other details can sometimes change.

Top Tier 2 Vendor Accounts (NO Personal Guarantee)

Advance Auto Parts

Advance Auto Parts sells replacement parts, performance parts, accessories, and fluids for vehicles.

If you're a commercial customer, you can register for their Advance Commercial Credit program. You must have at least five tradelines already set up for approval.

Advance Auto Parts reports to D&B.

Zoro

Zoro sells a very wide variety of products, including electronics, furniture, cleaning supplies, office supplies, and more.

They have a net 30 account that's available through Zoro Business Advantage (ZBA) and reports to D&B.

United Rentals

United Rentals is an industrial and construction equipment rental company.

You can apply for a trade credit account online or at your local United Rentals store. Note that the application does have room for an SSN, but it isn't required if you've been in business for at least two years.

United Rentals reports to Equifax.

Valero Fleet Card

A fleet card is used as a payment card for gasoline, diesel, and other fuels at gas stations. This particular one is accepted at over 5,000 Valero locations.

This is a credit card that allows you to carry a balance (note that carrying a balance isn't recommended when you're trying to build your credit), but can only be used at Valero. There are no setup, annual, or monthly fees. They report to D&B.

An alternative to the Valero Fleet Card is the ExxonMobil BusinessPro Fleet Card. As long as your business has been operational for at least a year, no personal guarantee is needed. They report to D&B and Experian.

HD Supply

HD Supply sells a wide variety of products, including cabinets, electronics, cleaning supplies, furniture, appliances, and more.

You can submit a trade credit application through their website. HD Supply reports to D&B.

Amazon Business

Amazon Business offers a corporate line of credit with net 55 terms and no annual fee. The credit line can be used for almost anything on Amazon, except for cell phones, textbook rentals, gift cards, and some digital items.

When you apply, you will be given the option to provide a personal guarantee. This is not required, as long as your company has been in business for at least two years and has a business credit history.

Amazon Business also has a Pay by Invoice option with net 30 terms. When you register for an Amazon Business account, you will be automatically assessed for Pay by Invoice. If you're approved, you will receive an invitation via email to activate the credit line.

Amazon Business reports to D&B.

From the list above, we highly recommend Zoro, HD Supply, and Amazon Business to most companies, as they sell a wide variety of products that nearly any business can benefit from. If you use a car or truck for any aspect of running your business, Advance Auto Parts and Valero or ExxonMobil fleet will also be useful. For those who need to rent large equipment for their business, United Rentals is a great choice.

Most businesses can easily receive tier 2 tradelines with any of the above vendors using an EIN only and no personal guarantee, as long as the business has been operational long enough with an established credit history via the tier 1 tradelines discussed in chapter 4.

Other Tier 2 Accounts

Some business owners may be aware that well-known retail stores, such as Staples, Home Depot, or Sam's Club, also offer tier 2 accounts that report to the major credit bureaus. The caveat is that you'll often need to provide a personal guarantee to receive a tier 2 account with these companies.

While many of these retail stores will waive the personal guarantee, your business must meet certain conditions. For example, to waive the personal guarantee with Staples, your business must be structured as a corporation, nonprofit, or government entity; have been in business for three years or longer; and have sales of at least $5 million.

Since small businesses don't generally fit these requirements, we recommend applying for the no personal guarantee tier 2 accounts listed in the previous section. You can also try applying to the retail stores listed here without providing an SSN, but just know that your approval odds are low, if you don't meet their minimum requirements for waiving the personal guarantee.

For those who are interested in applying, below are some additional tier 2 accounts that report to the major credit bureaus:

- *Staples* – reports to D&B
- *Home Depot* – reports to D&B, Equifax, and Experian
- *Lowe's* – reports to D&B
- *Office Depot* – reports to D&B
- *Sam's Club* – reports to Equifax and Experian (while this vendor doesn't report to D&B directly, it does report to TransUnion, which then forwards the data to D&B)

Many of the vendors above offer multiple types of business credit. Some are credit accounts, while others are store credit cards, which will typically offer more benefits and rewards.

Regardless of which ones you choose, the addition of 2–5 tier 2 tradelines with positive payment history to your profile will boost your credit score and increase your ability to receive higher levels of funding.

CHAPTER 6

Business Credit Cards

In this chapter, we'll explore the best business credit cards. No matter the size, scope, or industry of your business, you can find a card here that suits your needs.

While several of the tier 2 vendors in chapter 5 do offer credit cards, they're typically store-specific and have certain limitations. By contrast, the credit cards in this chapter will provide more flexibility, greater limits, and better rewards. Many of these cards even come with an expense management system, which is especially useful if your business has employees.

While some credit cards in this section are starter cards, others have more stringent requirements and likely won't be accessible when your business is just starting out. However, if you keep building your business via your tier 1 and tier 2 tradelines, you could eventually qualify for a card with better perks.

Note that the cards below don't let you carry a balance, meaning you must pay in full every month. This is preferable for building business credit and will help you earn a better score faster.

Unlike most business credit cards, you can apply to the ones listed below with just your EIN and no SSN required. As always, check the company websites for the most up-to-date information as terms and other details can change.

Top Business Credit Cards (NO Personal Guarantee)

Nav Prime Card

Nav Prime is a starter card that most new businesses will qualify for. You can even apply for this one alongside your tier 1 tradelines and use it right away.

This card helps you build business credit, even when you're first starting out, by reporting your payments as a monthly tradeline. This is the only commercial credit-building card with no business credit check or security deposit required.

It costs $49.99 per month and reports to all three of the major credit bureaus.

Divvy Visa (renamed BILL)

Divvy is a card with an expense report and budgeting system that rewards you for paying your bills early rather than on time. With Divvy, you can earn up to 7x points on restaurants, 5x on hotels, 2x on software subscriptions, and 1.5x on everything else.

Divvy does not check your business or personal credit score to determine eligibility for its card, which makes it easy for even new businesses to be approved.

There is no annual fee and Divvy reports to D&B, as well as the Small Business Finance Exchange (SBFE).

UPDATE: In September 2023, the Divvy card was rebranded to the BILL Divvy Corporate Card. It appears that with this change, an SSN may now be needed to apply for this card. While we've kept this card on the list, just in case requirements change, we now recommend the Expensify card instead, which we'll discuss next.

Expensify Corporate Card

Expensify is an expense management system that offers a corporate credit card. There is no personal liability or credit check required.

You'll need an Expensify account to get started. It takes just a few minutes to receive approval and expense tracking is automated within the system.

You can get 1% cash back with no restrictions and up to 4% cash back, if you meet certain conditions. You'll also qualify for discounts and exclusive perks from Expensify partners.

You can use the Expensify card anywhere that Visa is accepted.

Brex 30 Card

Brex has some of the best rewards among business cards that don't require a personal guarantee or credit check. The Brex card has no annual fee and offers up to 7x–8x points on a variety of purchases. It also offers limits that are 10–20 times higher than most traditional business credit cards.

The main downside is that while Brex used to be a great card for many new businesses, they now require start-ups to have funding secured to qualify for monthly payments. This limits the card primarily to venture-funded companies, alongside accelerator and angel-funded companies, that meet specific requirements. They also require a $50,000 minimum cash balance, unless you're referred by certain Brex partners.

Nevertheless, if you don't meet the criteria above, it could still be worth applying. You may still qualify for a Brex business account with daily payments.

Ramp Business Card

With Ramp, you can earn 1.5% cash back on all purchases. It has no annual fee.

To receive approval for the Ramp card, your business needs to be a corporation, LLC, or LLP with at least $75,000 in a US business bank account.

Stripe Corporate Card

This card is great for e-commerce businesses. It has no annual fee and offers unlimited 1.5% cash back on all purchases, alongside discounts and credits on a range of business tools and software.

To qualify, your business must be using Stripe payments already. If you have an online store, Stripe is a payment processing platform that allows you to accept online and credit card payments securely.

The Stripe Corporate card is available by invitation only (this could change later on). Currently, you can request an invitation through Stripe's beta program.

Other Business Credit Cards

All the cards above offer great perks and can be acquired with just your EIN and no personal guarantee. We recommend the Nav Prime Card to start since you can get it even when your business is new and it reports to all three credit bureaus.

If you're looking for even more options, this section presents a list of our other recommended business credit cards. The downside to these is that you will have to provide a personal guarantee, but unlike the ones listed in the previous section, you can carry a balance on them.

Just be aware that carrying a balance (even a small one) can negatively impact your credit score and negate certain rewards. For the best credit score, we recommend paying in full each month.

Here are some additional business credit cards that are great for small businesses:

- *Ink Business Unlimited* – Earn unlimited 1.5% cash back on purchases with no annual fee.

- *Blue Business Plus Card from American Express* – This card offers an introductory APR of 0% on purchases for the first 12 months. This can be an effective way to secure no-interest funding for your business. Just be sure to pay off the balance in full before the introductory period ends to rebuild your credit score and avoid any interest.

- *Bank of America Business Advantage Unlimited Cash Rewards Mastercard* – Earn 1.5% cash back on all purchases with no limits or expiration dates and no annual fee.

- *United MileagePlus Business Card* – This is a great card for those interested in travel and flight rewards. There is a $0 introductory annual fee for the first year and then the fee is $99 after that. It has great rewards and perks, such as 75,000 bonus miles, if you spend $5,000 in the first three months.

- *Amazon Business Prime American Express Card* – This is the ideal card for Prime members who make a lot of business purchases through Amazon. You'll earn 5% back on Amazon, 2% back at restaurants and gas stations, and 1% back on all other purchases with no annual fee.

Whether you choose a starter card, corporate card, or traditional business credit card, the rewards that you earn will help you build your business faster. Even 1% cash back adds up over time and will help your business grow.

Regardless of which business credit card you choose, remember to pay it off using your business bank account (not your personal one). This will ensure that your business and personal assets remain separate.

CHAPTER 7

Business Loans

In this chapter, we'll discuss how to get a business loan without a personal guarantee.

This can be a bit trickier than trade credit or credit cards. Most business loans require a personal guarantee, since they're very risky for the lender. This is especially true for unsecured loans that don't require collateral.

When it comes to pursuing a business loan without a personal guarantee, there are pros and cons for the borrower. The main benefit is that your personal assets will be safe, even if your business can't meet its debt obligations. If you provide a personal guarantee, the lender can go after your personal assets, including your house, car, and other possessions in your name.

On the flip side, if you don't provide a personal guarantee, your interest rates will likely be higher. You also may not be able to access higher funding amounts and your approval odds may be lower.

This is to say that every business is different and you should always do your research and consult with a professional regarding the best type of loan for your business.

Online Lenders

Most banks and traditional lenders won't issue a business loan without a personal guarantee. Instead, you'll need to pursue a loan with an online lender.

Online lenders typically have higher approval rates and can process the loan application quickly, sometimes as fast as 24 hours. On the flip side, online lenders often have higher interest rates than banks.

Here are some online lenders that offer unsecured (no collateral) business loans without a personal guarantee:

Upstart

This lender offers personal loans that can be used for business. No collateral, blanket lien, or personal guarantee is required. They are start-up friendly and offer repayment terms of up to five years.

The downside is that they may charge an origination fee of up to 12% to process your loan application.

Fundbox

This lender offers short-term loans for small businesses. There is no personal guarantee on most draws up to $50,000.

The downside is that they may require a blanket lien, which will still allow the lender to seize assets in the event of nonpayment.

National Business Capital

This is a business loan marketplace with over 75 lending partners. No personal guarantee is needed and there are no up-front fees.

The downside is that in order to apply, your business must have at least $120,000 in revenue per year. Even then, they generally only issue loans to businesses with an annual revenue of $480,000 or more.

Tips for Getting a Loan

In general, if you've followed the steps in this book, you should be in a good position to secure a business loan without a personal guarantee.

Before you apply for a business loan, be sure that:

- Your business is incorporated or registered as an LLC.
- Your business is professional and all information is consistent.
- You've built up a positive business credit history using tier 1 and tier 2 vendors.
- Your D&B PAYDEX score is at 80 or above.

When it comes to loans, it's important to do your research and shop around for the lender that best suits your business and needs. If you find that one lender requires a personal guarantee, there are always others to consider.

Businessloans.com and Lendio are online business loan marketplaces that allow you to compare loan offers from dozens of different lenders. Many of these lenders will require a personal guarantee, but some may not.

Most loans are open for discussion and negotiation. Creditworthiness, revenue, and time in business are all factors that are considered.

You can often negotiate with lenders to waive a personal guarantee or receive more favorable loan terms. You should also ask the lender if they report to the major credit bureaus, so you can keep building your credit as you repay the loan.

Be sure to always read any documents or terms carefully and consult with an expert if needed.

Other Funding Options

In this day and age, traditional and online lenders are not the only route to obtaining loans. In this section, we'll explore a few additional options for receiving loans or funding for your business without a personal guarantee that you may not have considered before.

Unlike traditional or online lenders, most of the options below aren't subject to approval or interest rates. Depending on your business, the alternatives on this list could be a more effective way for your company to receive the funding it needs.

Crowdfunding

Crowdfunding is when a "crowd" of individuals fund your business instead of just one or two lenders or investors.

There are five main kinds of crowdfunding:

- *Donation* – money given with nothing expected in return

- *Debt* – money given as a loan that must be repaid with interest by a specified deadline; also called peer-to-peer (P2P) lending and sometimes requires a personal guarantee

- *Reward* – money given in exchange for a reward, such as T-shirts or discounts

- *Equity* – money invested into companies and start-ups in exchange for equity

- *Subscription* – money given through an ongoing subscription fee, typically in exchange for content

Here are some crowdfunding platforms that will allow you to raise funds for your business:

- GoFundMe (donation)
- LendingClub (debt)
- Kickstarter (reward)
- StartEngine (equity)
- Patreon (subscription)

Rollovers as Business Start-Ups (ROBS)

This is a plan that moves money from a retirement account, such as a 401(k), into your business without incurring taxes or early withdrawal fees.

This can be used as an alternative to other small business loans allowing you to fund your own business with no collateral, risk to your personal assets, or need for lender approval. Benetrends and Guidant Financial are well-respected ROBS providers.

Just be aware that you're using your own retirement savings to fund your business, which comes with its own set of risks. For this reason, you should consult with a financial advisor before pursuing this option.

Angel Investing

Most people think of angel investors as wealthy individuals who invest money into start-ups in exchange for equity. These are essentially unsecured loans since the investor has no claim on the company's assets.

The easiest way to find this kind of angel investor is through AngelList, a large database that allows you to filter your search by location, industry, and more. After creating a profile for your business, you can raise funds from angel investors for free. You can also find angel investors by networking on LinkedIn or attending industry events.

Also bear in mind that an angel investor can be nearly anyone who is willing and able to help fund your business. This can include friends, family members, local professionals, and others. Keep an open mind and you may discover worthwhile loan or funding opportunities that you didn't see before.

CHAPTER 8

Insider Tips

In this chapter, we'll present our final must-know tips and recommendations for effectively building your business credit.

By following these tips alongside the other steps in this book, you'll establish a strong business credit profile and score. This will ensure you qualify for the trade credit, credit cards, and loans you'll need to successfully grow your business.

1. Open a Business Bank Account

Once you've formed your LLC or corporation and have an EIN, you should immediately open a business bank account.

While this doesn't directly contribute to establishing business credit, it's simply good practice to keep your business and personal finances separate. Be sure that all your business income and expenses flow through this account only—this will be a huge help come tax season!

Some business lenders even require a business bank account before they'll issue credit or a loan, so it's just generally good to have. It will make your business appear more professional and creditworthy.

2. Make Payments Early

Payment history is a hugely important factor in determining your business credit score. While on-time payments are essential, early payments are preferred.

It shows potential creditors and lenders that your business has cash flow and will help you achieve higher limits and better terms without a personal guarantee.

With D&B PAYDEX, in particular, you'll earn the highest score by paying early. In fact, it's possible to increase your PAYDEX score to 90 or higher by paying your invoices 10–20 days before their due date.

3. Strive to Pay in Full

While certain vendor accounts and credit cards let you carry a balance, you should always strive to pay in full every month. Just paying the minimum isn't enough if you want to achieve the optimal business credit score.

To that end, you should always be responsible with your credit. Never charge more than your business can comfortably pay back within the payment terms.

4. Keep Your Credit Utilization Low

Credit utilization is how much credit you've used compared to how much credit is available to you.

Most credit experts recommend keeping your credit utilization below 30% to maintain a strong credit score. As an example, if your credit lines total $10,000, you should try not to exceed $3,000 in outstanding balances.

Some vendors don't report credit utilization to the bureaus, but many do. It's not as large a factor in determining your credit score as early payments or paying in full, but nevertheless, it's still good practice to keep your credit utilization as low as possible.

While D&B's PAYDEX focuses primarily on payment history, Equifax and Experian scores measure credit risk, which is affected by credit utilization.

In addition, some lenders will look through your credit history manually and take into account your credit utilization when making approval decisions. If you're looking to be approved for credit with no personal guarantee, it's important not to give lenders any reason to worry about how you manage your debt.

5. Use Your Credit Continuously

If you want to build a strong business credit profile and score, you'll need to use your available credit continuously. Simply getting approved for a vendor account does nothing to build your credit, if you aren't consistently using the trade credit and paying it off in a timely manner.

You should regularly place orders with your vendor accounts to keep those tradelines active and growing. This shows other potential lenders that you can effectively utilize and manage your credit.

While you can grow your business credit quickly, be aware that time is also a factor. The longer history you have of paying back your debts on time or early, the less risky you'll appear to potential lenders and creditors. This will help you obtain better approval odds, higher credit limits, and more favorable terms.

A seasoned tradeline is a credit account that has been active for at least two years with a positive payment history. You should strive to have at least 5–10 of these on your credit report over time. In order to achieve this, you must keep even your oldest tradelines open and reporting consistent activity.

While not strictly necessary, lenders also like to see a diverse mix of credit on your profile, including trade credit, revolving credit (credit cards), loans, and even leases. This shows that your business is able to manage different types of credit responsibly, which can decrease risk in the eyes of lenders.

6. Request Credit Limit Increases

You can often request higher limits after six months of positive payment history. This will allow you to make larger purchases, while keeping your credit utilization low.

As stated previously, just make sure you can comfortably pay off your debts in full each month, preferably early, before you start increasing spending for your business.

With these proven tips, you'll build a strong business credit profile in no time! Just stick with it and remember to set up credit monitoring and keep an eye on your reports (see chapter 3). This will help you track your progress, as well as show you any areas where improvements can be made.

Bonus: Credit Building Resource List

If you'd like a FREE clickable list of all the resources mentioned in this book, go to boundlessbooks.ck.page/credit and sign up!

This helpful bonus provides links to all the websites you'll need for setting up credit monitoring, applying to tier 1 and tier 2 vendor accounts, accessing business credit cards, comparing business loans, and so much more!

This will save you a TON of valuable time, so you don't have to search for it all on your own.

Once you sign up, we'll deliver the list straight to your inbox. You'll also receive occasional emails from us with business tips and new book releases.

Conclusion

Congrats! You've made it to the end and are ready to receive funding for your business using your EIN, while also building your business credit score like a pro.

We have complete confidence that the insider guidance in this book will give you a unique advantage when pursuing business credit. By having access to information that others don't, you'll already be several steps ahead and can command funding for your business with assurance.

Before we end, here's a quick review of the steps outlined in this book:

1. Register your business by forming an LLC or corporation.

2. Ensure that your business is professional and consistent across the board so that it appears fundable to both creditors and lenders.

3. Register for a DUNS (plus set up your profile with D&B), access your business credit reports, and sign up for credit monitoring. Keep in mind that you may need a minimum of three tradelines before your scores are generated.

4. Receive approval for at least 5–8 tier 1 vendor accounts that will report your net 30 tradelines to the main credit bureaus.

5. After 90 days or more of positive payment history for your tier 1 accounts have been reported, increase your tradelines with 2–5 tier 2 accounts.

6. Apply for business credit cards, loans, and other funding, as needed.

7. Strive to always pay early and in full, while using your credit continuously and keeping your credit utilization low. After six months of positive payment history, you can qualify for higher limits.

Thanks for reading and good luck with your business. We wish you all the success in the world!

If you found this book helpful, could you please leave a quick review or rating on Amazon? This means the world to us and helps the right readers find our book!

References

Berry, T. (2023). "The Four Tiers of Small Business Financing."
Retrieved from https://www.bplans.com/business-
funding/options/financing-tiers/.

Best, R. (2023). "Best ROBS Providers." Retrieved from
https://www.investopedia.com/best-robs-providers-5084864.

Camberato, J. (2023). "Can I get an Unsecured Business Loan With
No Personal Guarantee?" Retrieved from
https://www.nationalbusinesscapital.com/blog/unsecured-business-
loan-with-no-personal-guarantee/.

Detweiler, G. (2023). "22 Easy Approval Net-30 Accounts to Build
Business Credit." Retrieved from https://www.nav.com/resource/net-
30-accounts/.

Detweiler, G. (2023). "How to Build Your Business Credit Fast."
Retrieved from https://www.nav.com/resource/how-to-establish-
business-credit/.

Dieker, N. (2023). "Everything You Need to Know About Credit
Utilization Ratio." Retrieved from
https://www.bankrate.com/finance/credit-cards/credit-utilization-ratio/.

Gobler, E. (2022). "What is an Amazon Business Line of Credit and
is it right for you?" Retrieved from
https://www.zdnet.com/finance/amazon-business-line-of-credit-review/.

Murphy, R. (2023). "What Are Rollovers as Business Startups (ROBS)?" Retrieved from https://www.nerdwallet.com/article/small-business/rollovers-as-business-startups-robs.

Nelson, B. (2023). "What is a Good Business Credit Score?" Retrieved from https://www.nav.com/resource/what-is-a-good-business-credit-score/.

Planning Guides. (2023). "Net 30 Vendors that Report to DNB, Experian, Equifax & More." Retrieved from https://planning.net/business/credit/vendors/reporting/.

Planning Guides. (2023). "Tier 2 Business Credit Vendors, No PG Cards & Tradelines." Retrieved from https://planning.net/business/credit/vendors/tier/2/.

Stewart, F. (2023). "The Truth About Business Funding With No Personal Guarantee Credit." Retrieved from https://www.creditsuite.com/blog/no-personal-guarantee-credit/.

Stewart, F. (2022). "Why Your Business Address Matters." Retrieved from https://www.creditsuite.com/blog/business-address/.

TRUiC Team. (2023). "14 Best Angel Investor Websites for Startups in 2023." Retrieved from https://startupsavant.com/startup-center/best-angel-investor-websites.

Vissers, S. (2023). "8 Best Unsecured Business Loans." Retrieved from https://www.merchantmaverick.com/best-unsecured-business-loans/.

Titles by Alyssa and Garrett Garner

Start a Craft Business Series:

Etsy Business Launch: The Complete Guide to Making Six Figures Selling on Etsy

Candle Making Business: How to Launch a Thriving Six-Figure Candle Business from Home

Business Fundamentals Series:

The Insider's Guide to Business Credit Using an EIN Only: Get Tradelines, Credit Cards, and Loans for Your Business with No Personal Guarantee

LLC Guide – Coming Soon!

Other Business Books:

Launch Your Notary Public and Loan Signing Agent Business: The Ultimate Guide to Starting a Thriving Six-Figure Notary Business (Even If You're a Total Beginner) – Coming Soon!

About the Authors

Alyssa and Garrett are married entrepreneurs with almost a decade of experience in the online business space. They've dabbled in everything from blogging and e-commerce to publishing and real estate.

Over the years, they've discovered a practical and reproducible framework for building highly profitable businesses in a short amount of time. Now, their passion lies in teaching budding entrepreneurs how to escape the grind and find financial freedom doing what they love.

When they're not building their entrepreneurial empire, Alyssa and Garrett enjoy travel, ballroom dancing, and Broadway shows.

Thanks for reading!

www.ingramcontent.com/pod-product-compliance
Lightning Source LLC
Chambersburg PA
CBHW060004300526
45794CB00003B/1074